AF593708

PANZERS IN RUSSIA 1943-45

PzKpfw IVHs retreat during the winter of 1943–44 (277/843/3).

A selection of German wartime photographs
from the Bundesarchiv, Koblenz

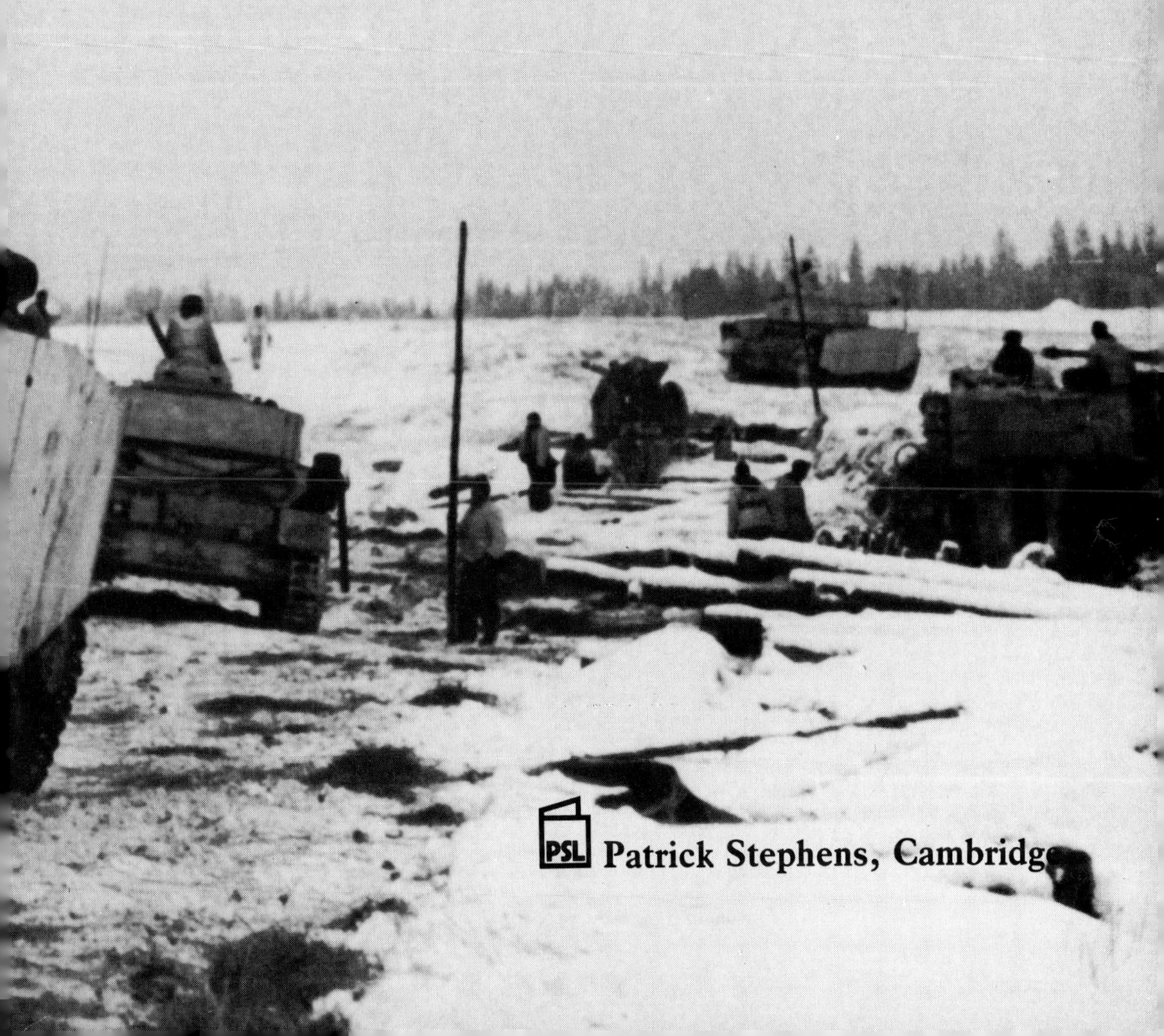

PSL Patrick Stephens, Cambridge

First published in 1979

British Library Cataloguing in Publication Data

Panzers in Russia, 1943-45. – (World War 2 photo albums; 12).
1. Germany. Heer – History
2.World War, 1939-1945 – Campaigns – Russia – Pictorial works
3. Tanks (Military science) – History – Pictorial works
I. Quarrie, Bruce II. Series
940.54'21 D757.54

ISBN 0 85059 387 5 (casebound)
ISBN 0 85059 389 1 (softbound)

Photoset in 10pt Plantin Roman. Printed in Great Britain on 100 gsm Pedigree coated cartridge and bound by The Garden City Press Limited, Letchworth, Hertfordshire SG6 1JS, for the publishers, Patrick Stephens Limited, Bar Hill, Cambridge, CB3 8EL, England.

CONTENTS

Acknowledgements
The author and publisher would like to express their sincere thanks to Mrs Marianne Loenartz of the Bundesarchiv for her assistance, without which this book would have been impossible.

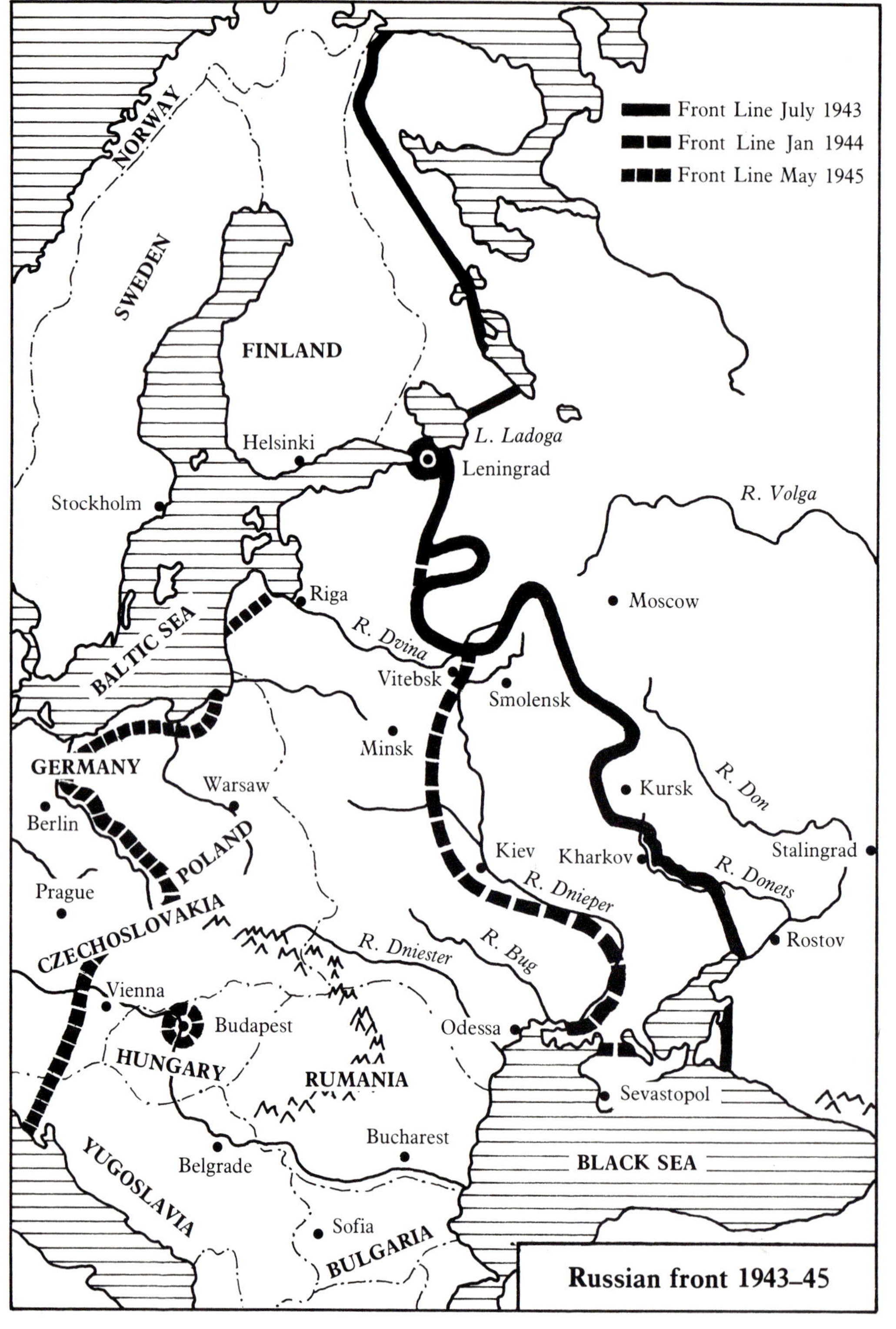

Russian front 1943–45

AUTHOR'S INTRODUCTION

Following the disaster at Stalingrad and the Soviet Army's sweeping 1943 winter offensive (see Nos 3 and 9 in this series), the German ground forces were sent reeling westwards and only managed to stem the tide in March. At this point, however, following the recapture of Kharkov by Hausser's SS Panzer Korps, they were actually in a stronger position than they had been whilst advancing the previous summer, as their front line was considerably shorter. Moreover, increasing numbers of more heavily armed and armoured tanks – including the Tiger – were reaching the Panzer divisions, and the new Panther was about to make its debut.

There were two significant features in the front line at the beginning of April: a German salient centred around Orel and a larger Soviet salient to its south, around Kursk. The German Staff were not long in coming to the conclusion that a successful summer 1943 offensive aimed – at long last – at capturing Moscow could not be launched without first 'pinching off' this ulcer in their flank. Plans were therefore put in hand for a two-pronged encirclement on a narrow front from both north and south, in which it was hoped the Soviet forces around Kursk would be trapped.

However, the Russians were equally quick to see the vital importance of their positions here, and began heavily reinforcing them at the same time as the Germans were beginning their own build-up. Marshal Zhukov recommended a strong defence in depth against which the German forces would wear themselves down, followed by a counter-attack when they were suitably exhausted. This plan was criticised in some quarters since it was felt wrong to hand the Germans the initiative on a plate, whilst others felt strongly that attack was still the best means of defence. Tactically, the Marshal was to be proved wrong, but luckily for him other political and strategic factors were to come into play to save the Soviet forces.

South of the Kursk salient, where the main effort was to be concentrated, the Germans amassed under Manstein the 3rd, 6th, 7th, 11th and 19th Panzer Divisions, Panzer-Grenadier Division 'Grossdeutschland', the 1st SS Panzer Division Leibstandarte 'Adolf Hitler', 2nd SS Panzer Division 'Das Reich' and 3rd SS Panzer Division 'Totenkopf'. Hoth, commanding 4th Panzer Army, took control of the 3rd and 11th Panzer Divisions, 'Grossdeutschland' and the three SS divisions, whilst the 6th, 7th and 19th Panzer Divisions fell under Kempf. They were reinforced by three infantry divisions each. Hoth also took under command von Lauchert's brigade of the new PzKpfw V Ausf D (Panzerabteilungen 51 and 52). Von Knobelsdorff was in command of this unit and the three army divisions in XLVIII Panzer Korps, Hausser the three divisions of II SS Panzer Korps, and Breith Kempf's three Panzer divisions.

In the north von Kluge deployed Model's 9th Army with only six Panzer divisions (supported by 12 infantry divisions and the 10th Panzer-Grenadier Division) in the front line and two in reserve. Harpe's XLI Panzer Korps comprised the latter together with the 18th Panzer Division; Lemelsen's XLVII Panzer Korps was strongest, comprising the 2nd, 4th, 9th, 20th and 24th Panzer Divisions, with the 5th and 12th in reserve; while Zorn's XLVI Korps was a 'Panzer' unit in name only, containing solely infantry formations.

These dispositions reflect both the differing military attitudes and abilities of Kluge and Manstein, and the different solutions each had arrived at for dealing with the strong Soviet defensive positions. These were formidable. There were six belts of defences, deployed in places to a depth of 110 miles, consisting of dug-in anti-tank, mortar and machine-gun strongpoints well sited to take on those German armoured units which succeeded in breaking through the extremely dense minefields into prepared 'killing grounds'. As many as 12 anti-tank guns were deployed in single batteries, although five was the average. The minefields had a density of 2,400 anti-tank and 2,700 anti-personnel mines per mile of front*.

**The Russian Front*, edited by James F. Dunnigan (Arms and Armour Press, 1978).

Where the Russians miscalculated was in their assessment of the main assault's direction, which they were convinced would fall in the north. As a result, Rokossovsky faced Model with six Armies (each equivalent to a German Korps), giving him a three to two superiority in numbers without counting the massive reserve artillery support; while in the south Vatutin's five Armies were effectively outnumbered by six to five. In fact the odds here were even more in the Germans' favour as they were to concentrate their attack on a very narrow front – less than 30 miles – which meant their entire might fell on just two of Vatutin's Armies. However, Zhukov, the Russian Fox, had kept a very strong mobile reserve, equivalent to four German Korps, one of them armoured.

The final line-up gave the German forces 2,700 tanks and assault guns against a Russian total of 3,300; 900,000 infantry versus 1,337,000; 10,000 artillery pieces versus no fewer than 20,220 Russian guns; and 2,500 support aircraft, including the tank-busting Hs 129, against 2,650 Soviet machines*.

The German attack was originally scheduled for June 12, but the Axis collapse in North Africa (see No 1 in this series) and fears of an imminent invasion of southern Europe made Hitler postpone it for three weeks. Unusually, for most attacks are launched at dawn, the offensive opened at 1500 hours on July 4, in the south.

Here, Manstein's tactics against the Soviet defences were based on the 'Panzerkeil' concept – massive armoured wedges headed by the heavy Tiger tanks and the new Elefant SP guns, followed and flanked by the lighter PzKpfw IVs and Panthers, followed in turn by the mechanised infantry units and finally by the slower-moving 'foot-sloggers'. Hoth's 4th Panzer Army opened the attack by moving against the Soviet-controlled higher ground overlooking its positions. This they accomplished with some difficulty.

On the 5th the offensive opened in earnest. In the north, Model's infantry-heavy forces were utilising different tactics whereby the infantry went in first to clear the anti-tank gun nests, followed by the armour. In this way the XLVI Panzer Korps succeeded in dislodging the Russian 15th Rifle Division, but elsewhere progress was extremely slow and hampered by a Russian artillery bombardment during the night of the 4th/5th which somewhat disrupted German preparations.

Kursk, by Geoffrey Jukes (Macdonald, 1969).

On July 6 both German pincers made encouraging headway. Model began committing his armour to exploit the breach in the 15th Rifle Division's positions and reached the high ground north of Kashara. Here, however, it was stalled, and a see-saw armoured battle involving over 1,100 tanks and assault guns on each side developed which was to last four days. In the south, von Knobelsdorff made good headway, the 'Grossdeutschland' Division justifying its reputation as the Army's elite by capturing the village of Dubrova and forcing the Russian 3rd Mechanised Corps back to the line of the River Pena, the last obstacle before the important town of Oboyan, which Vatutin had ordered held at all costs.

Hausser's tough SS divisions had also made good progress on the 6th, penetrating some 20 miles towards Prokhorovka. However, despite the fact that the Russian line was now breached significantly in two places, Kempf's detachment, which was supposed to provide flank cover for the SS divisions, had only been able to make slow headway after crossing the River Donets and was stalled by Shumilov's 7th Guards Army.

At the end of the day the Germans had cause for some optimism, although losses had been high both amongst the tanks, and the infantry, where the Russian artillery superiority had proved its value. The new Panther tanks had also proved something of a disappointment, although a large part of this was due to the fact that von Lauchert's brigade became entangled in a minefield early in the day and could only extricate itself with difficulty. In the south they had also confused the Russians by swinging towards Prokhorovka instead of continuing to head due north as had been anticipated.

On Model's northern front the next few days were a nightmare. Russian reinforcements seemed to materialise wherever the Germans attacked – east or west. Securely dug-in on higher ground, virtually all the Soviets had to do was wait for the Panzers to come at them, then hack them to pieces. German reserves in this sector dwindled rapidly, although after the capture of the village of Teploye on the 8th by 4th Panzer Division a breakthrough seemed imminent. However, the ridge behind was defended in strength and, although it changed hands three times, the Germans were unable to exploit this local success. To the east of this position, the village of Ponyri became a 'miniature Stalingrad' with every building turned into a stronghold and, again, the Germans were unable to break through. Moreover, having stabilised the Kursk situation, the Russians were themselves now opening an attack on the Orel salient. . .

In the south a similar see-saw situation developed, although the 'Grossdeutschland' division in particular experienced considerable success, as did the SS formations (see 'Vanguard' 2 and 7 by the same author [Osprey, 1977 and 1979]). On July 10 Panzer Regiment 6 (3rd Panzer Division) made significant progress across the River Pena, then turned into the rear of the 71st Guards Rifle Division and rolled it up, whilst 'Grossdeutschland' and the 11th Panzer Division pushed all before them to take the high ground overlooking Oboyan and the River Psel. However, here they were stopped because a crucial battle was developing in Hausser's sector to their east, and they were required for flank support.

The battle at this point hung in the balance; although the German forces were seriously depleted, their immediate Soviet opponents were in even worse state, the 6th Guards Army being particularly demoralised. However, the Germans now had their eyes – figuratively speaking – over their shoulders as news of the Allied landings in Sicily reached them; Hitler was vacillating as usual; and 5th Guards Tank Army had arrived after a 225-mile march to reinforce the Russian front.

The largest single tank battle of the war opened on July 12 between the latter formation and Hausser's SS Panzer Korps as the Soviets finally launched a strong counterattack. Some Russian tanks – mostly T–34s – engaged the 700-odd PzKpfw IVs and Tigers of Hausser's command. For much of the day the fighting was literally at point-blank range, the lines of tanks interpenetrating and blasting away at each other with every weapon available. Overhead, the Red air force battled desperately with the Luftwaffe for command of the skies. Great courage, determination and, indeed, fanaticism was displayed by the tank crews of both nationalities, but the end result was almost a second Borodino: Rotmistrov's tanks failed to destroy the SS Panzer Korps as planned and had to retire from the field of battle; but with nearly half his armoured forces eliminated, Hausser was in no position to exploit this very Phyrric victory. Operation 'Zitadelle' (the German code name for the battle) was, to all intents and purposes, over. The Fuhrer wanted to disengage the SS units and send them to Italy, and Manstein – who claimed with some possible justification that one more effort by XLVIII Panzer Korps would tip the scales – was told to call his dogs off. Moreover, the long-expected Russian counter-offensive against the Orel salient was beginning to unfold, and Model was in danger of being outflanked and taken in the rear. By the 13th the Soviets had penetrated 16 miles into the German defences, and Model withdrew his forces.

Now the Russians really began applying pressure. To the south of Kharkov they attacked 1st Panzer Army and the new 6th Army, whilst Vatutin drove a wedge between Hoth and Kempf. The SS Korps was kept busy rushing from one sector to the other to try to stabilise the situation, but to no avail. Kharkov, which Hitler had ordered held at all costs, was practically surrounded and by mid-August Manstein was forced to make a unilateral decision to abandon the city. At the same time the Soviets broke through 6th Army's positions on the River Msus and headed for the Donets basin with the evident intent of cutting off those German troops remaining in the Crimea. At the end of August Hitler was forced to agree to pull back the whole line some 40 miles to a new, hastily improvised, defensive position. 17th Army was withdrawn from its foothold on the Kuban peninsular into the Crimea.

But the Russians were now in full cry and, on September 6, broke through these new positions, threatening Kiev. By the middle of the month it had become obvious even to Hitler that, unless Manstein was allowed to withdraw his entire front behind the River Dnepr, the Russians would have penetrated so far that even this line would be untenable. The race was now on, for the Dnepr is the most western defensive line in Russia, covering not only the ore-producing area south of Kiev which was vital to the German war machine, but also open access to Rumania and southern Poland.

The Russians and the Germans reached the Dnepr practically simultaneously but, for some reason best known to themselves, the Soviets did not contest the major bridge crossings, contenting themselves with small local crossings by boat which the Germans were able to repulse with ease. A large-scale airborne drop by night had the misfortune to land in the middle of XXIV Panzer Korps' deployment area and was decimated. Only in one place did the Russians secure a bridgehead west of the river, near Kiev, at the end of September. Vatutin rapidly reinforced this and began building up for a renewed offensive, which opened on November 3. Kiev fell, followed by Zaporozhye and Melitopol, and 17th Army was cut off in the Crimea.

These operations set the tone for the remainder of the campaign: however valiantly they fought, the German forces were pushed inexorably westward, the initiative being entirely in Russian hands.

The winter 1944 campaign opened on January 5 with a two-pronged encirclement around Kirovgrad which trapped four divisions, including 3rd and 14th Panzer. Fortunately they were led by Fritz Bayerlein, who had been with Rommel in North Africa, and he succeeded in breaking out and stabilising the line. However, worse was to come. Towards the end of January a similar operation, but on a larger scale, succeeded in trapping some nine divisions, including SS 'Wiking', amounting to 56,000 men, in the so-called Cherkassy Pocket. Here, however, Hitler ordered a rescue operation (unlike Stalingrad, where he had left von Paulus to his fate). Nine Panzer divisions were assigned to this but one, the 24th, had to be detached to meet a Soviet breakthrough further south, around Nikopol

The relief operation opened during the night of February 11/12 and, by the 15th, only three miles separated the rescuers from the forces in the pocket. Here they were stalled and the final effort had to be made by the frozen and exhausted men in the encirclement. They broke out during the night of the 16th/17th and the two groups linked hands. By the 19th the surviving 35,000 men had been extricated – but had been forced to abandon most of their heavy equipment.

On March 4 Zhukov attacked Manstein's northern flank and broke through 4th Panzer Army, while on the 5th Koniev decimated 8th Army and, pushing on rapidly, was soon across the River Bug, then the Dnestr, before wheeling north to encircle 1st Panzer Army. The usual arguments between Hitler and the commander on the spot then ensued: hold or break out and re-group. This time Manstein lost and was relieved of his command. In typical paranoid fashion, Hitler was continuing to replace his most efficient subordinates with 'yes-men'. However, there was nothing ineffectual about Hube, now left in charge, and 1st Panzer's attempt was successful, despite the fact that Zhukov threw his 11th Guard Tank Corps into the fray. After desperate fighting during the latter days of March, the SS Division 'Frundsberg' managed to open the route to safety on April 6.

Whilst the major operations continued in the south, the Russians had also re-opened the Leningrad front in the middle of January 1944. Attacking in the vicinity of Lake Ilmen, they drove the German lines back some 50 miles to a position centred around Vitebsk.

Apart from further operations during April which compressed the 17th Army into an ever-decreasing perimeter around Sevastopol, the spring 'muddy' period saw a general respite in the fighting and a regrouping for the Soviet summer offensive. Unexpectedly, this fell on Army Group Centre, which had been left relatively untouched during the earlier battles of 1944, and once again it was totally successful. Launched on June 22 – the third anniversary of the campaign – it involved a quarter of a million Russian troops against less than a sixth this number of Germans: 3rd Panzer Army was assaulted either side of Vitebsk, 4th Army between Orsha and Mogilev, and 9th Army in the Brobruisk area. The divisional-sized German 'hedgehogs' around these centres were bypassed and isolated and, within a week, the whole German front had collapsed. Minsk fell on July 3, Vilna a week later and Lublin on the 24th. Two days later the Russian forces under Rokossovsky reached the River Vistula and the Germans abandoned Brest-Litovsk. By the end of the month it looked as though the war was all but over.

Now, however, the picture altered. Russian troops were exhausted and their tanks badly in need of maintenance, having covered 450 miles in just over a month. Moreover, despite the almost total destruction of Army Group Centre, German resistance was stiffening as they were pushed further west and, of course, their lines of communication and supply were becoming much shorter. The focus thus returned to the south.

Here, the Germans' Rumanian allies were becoming increasingly half-hearted about the whole campaign and, when the Russians attacked on August 20, they fled back behind the River Danube. . .at which point Antonescu capitulated and changed sides, leaving 16 German divisions trapped to be destroyed. Rumania was occupied by the end of the month and Russia then declared war on Bulgaria – which also capitulated promptly. The next objective was Hungary, Tito having diplomatically persuaded Stalin not to invade Yugoslavia.

The assault into Hungary opened at the end of October and the Germans (with their Hungarian allies) were rapidly pushed back to Budapest, which was completely encircled by Christmas.

Offensive operations during 1944 ended in the north, where a Russian attack on October 5 had forced the Germans to abandon Riga. At the end of the year the remnants of Army Group North were cut off within Courland, the northern part of Latvia, and the Memel bridgehead.

The Russians paused only two weeks to catch their breath and reorganise. Thanks to Hitler's Ardennes offensive (see No 5 in this series) and his diversion of the 4th SS Panzer Korps to the relief of Budapest, they enjoyed something like an overall 13 to one superiority. Huge wedges were driven into Poland, where Zhukov entered Warsaw on January 17, and a foothold gained in East Prussia. On the 22nd Koniev reached the River Oder, while Rokossovsky had captured Tannenburg on the 20th and was on the Gulf of Danzig by the 26th. Zhukov reached Brandenburg, a mere 100 miles from Berlin, at the end of the month.

To all intents and purposes, Germany had now lost the war, but still Hitler persisted in his mad daydream. 6th Panzer Army was redeployed to the relief of Budapest after the failure of the Ardennes offensive, but the Russians were more interested in destroying Germany than Hungary.

Pressing his advantage, Zhukov crossed the River Oder during the first week of February, followed by Koniev, taking the Russian forces to within 40 miles of Berlin.

The last German offensive of the war, designed optimistically to cut off Zhukov's spearheads in Pomerania and Silesia, was doomed to failure – partly because it lacked strength due to so many armoured formations being detached to the relief of Budapest, and partly because of uninspired leadership. However, it gave Zhukov pause for thought (he had not believed the Germans capable of mounting any form of counterattack) and, instead of heading straight for Berlin, he spent the remainder of the month consolidating his position.

However, on February 24 Rokossovsky attacked northwards towards Danzig, and a week later reached the Baltic coast. Danzig, with a long history of sieges, however, managed to hold out until the end of March. Meanwhile, Zhukov had smashed 3rd Panzer Army, while Koniev proceeded to clear Upper Silesia almost at leisure.

Despite the fact that Budapest had fallen on February 23, consigning 100,000 German soldiers to a captivity from which many would never return, Hitler continued with his insane 'relief' operation, which was spearheaded by 2nd and 6th Panzer Armies. (Although this sounds impressive, it should be remembered that, by this stage of the war, most German units were only a fraction of their theoretical establishment.)

However, Tolbukhin was ready for them. The attack got off to a bad start on March 6 due to freezing weather and 6th Panzer

Army's unpreparedness, then bogged down on the 7th thanks to a sudden thaw. After six days' fighting the Germans had only succeeded in advancing some five miles, and by the middle of the month the attack had run out of steam. Tolbukhin then counter-attacked in strength, his objective: Vienna. By April 4 he was on Austrian soil and three days later entered the capital. The city surrendered on the 13th. At the same time, in the north, the East Prussian capital, Königsberg, was also invested, surrendering on the 10th.

German morale was understandably low, since everybody except Hitler now knew the war was irrevocably lost. But the last act still had to be played out.

Zhukov spent two weeks at the beginning of April redeploying his forces in front of Berlin, amassing a quarter of a million men and over 6,000 tanks in three Fronts. This was really using a sledgehammer to crack a nut. The German forces were under strength, low in ammunition, and their ranks padded with young boys and old men from the Volkssturm.

The Russian hammer fell on April 16. To their surprise the German lines did not immediately break, although they were forced to give ground. Regardless of the politics of the system they were fighting for, one cannot help feeling admiration for the courage and tenacity of the average German soldier under these conditions. However, the end could not be long delayed.

During the 18th/19th Koniev pushed across the River Spree and German defences north of Berlin melted away. In the centre, 9th Army still held firm, but to the south the Russians pushed across the lower Oder. Soviet Troops were thus behind 9th Army's line and its commander, Busse, requested permission to fall back; permission which Hitler characteristically denied.

On April 20, Hitler's birthday, 4th Panzer Army – or what was left of it – pulled off a local counter-attack which Hitler took as a sign from the gods that victory was nigh! The gods decreed otherwise. The following day the Russians had entered the Berlin suburbs and a day later the courageous 9th Army was assured of encirclement. Berlin was encompassed on the 25th, the same day that Soviet and American troops linked hands on the River Elbe. An attempted relief operation failed, and bitter fighting continued inside the city as the Russians tightened the ring. The Reichstag was taken on April 30 and the hammer and sickle flew triumphantly over Berlin. Hitler committed suicide and, on May 1, the city surrendered. Six days later Grand Admiral Dönitz surrendered the whole country. The war in Europe was over but its repercussions continue to the present day.

ABOUT THE PHOTOGRAPHS

The photographs in this book have been selected with care from the Bundesarchiv, Koblenz (the approximate German equivalent of the US National Archives or the British Public Records Office). Particular attention has been devoted to choosing photographs which will be fresh to the majority of readers, although it is inevitable that one or two may be familiar. Other than this, the author's prime concern has been to choose good-quality photographs which illustrate the type of detail that enthusiasts and modellers require. In certain instances quality has, to a degree, been sacrificed in order to include a particularly interesting photograph. For the most part, however, the quality speaks for itself.

The Bundesarchiv files hold some one million black and white negatives of Wehrmacht and Luftwaffe subjects, including 150,000 on the Kriegsmarine, some 20,000 glass negatives from the inter-war period and several hundred colour photographs. Sheer numbers is one of the problems which makes the compilation of a book such as this difficult. Other difficulties include the fact that, in the vast majority of cases, the negatives have not been printed so the researcher is forced to look through box after box of 35 mm contact strips – some 250 boxes containing an average of over 5,000 pictures each, plus folders containing a further 115,000 contact prints of the Waffen-SS; moreover, cataloguing and indexing the negatives is neither an easy nor a short task, with the result that, at the present time, Luftwaffe and Wehrmacht subjects as well as entirely separate theatres of operations are intermingled in the same files.

There is a simple explanation for this confusion. The Bundesarchiv photographs were taken by war correspondents attached to German military units, and the negatives were originally stored in the Reich Propaganda Ministry in Berlin. Towards the close of World War 2, all the photographs – then numbering some 3½ million – were ordered to be destroyed. One man in the Ministry, a Herr Evers, realised that they should be preserved for posterity and, acting entirely unofficially and on his own initiative, commandeered the first available suitable transport – two refrigerated fish trucks – loaded the negatives into them, and set out for safety. Unfortunately, one of the trucks disappeared en route and, to this day, nobody knows what happened to it. The remainder were captured by the Americans and shipped to Washington, where they remained for 20 years before the majority were returned to the government of West Germany. A large number, however, still reside in Washington. Thus the Bundesarchiv files are incomplete, with infuriating gaps for any researcher. Specifically, they end in the autumn of 1944, after Arnhem, and thus record none of the drama of the closing months of the war.

The photographs are currently housed in a modern office block in Koblenz, overlooking the River Mosel. The priceless negatives are stored in the basement, and there are strict security checks on anyone seeking admission to the Bildarchiv (Photo Archive). Regrettably, and the author has been asked to stress this point, the archives are *only open to bona fide authors and publishers, and prints can only be supplied for reproduction in a book or magazine*. They CANNOT be supplied to private collectors or enthusiasts for personal use, so *please* – don't write to the Bundesarchiv or the publishers of this book asking for copy prints, because they cannot be provided. The well-equipped photo laboratory at the Bundesarchiv is only capable of handling some 80 to 100 prints per day because each is printed individually under strictly controlled conditions – another reason for the fine quality of the photographs but also a contributory factor in the above legislation.

THE PHOTOGRAPHS

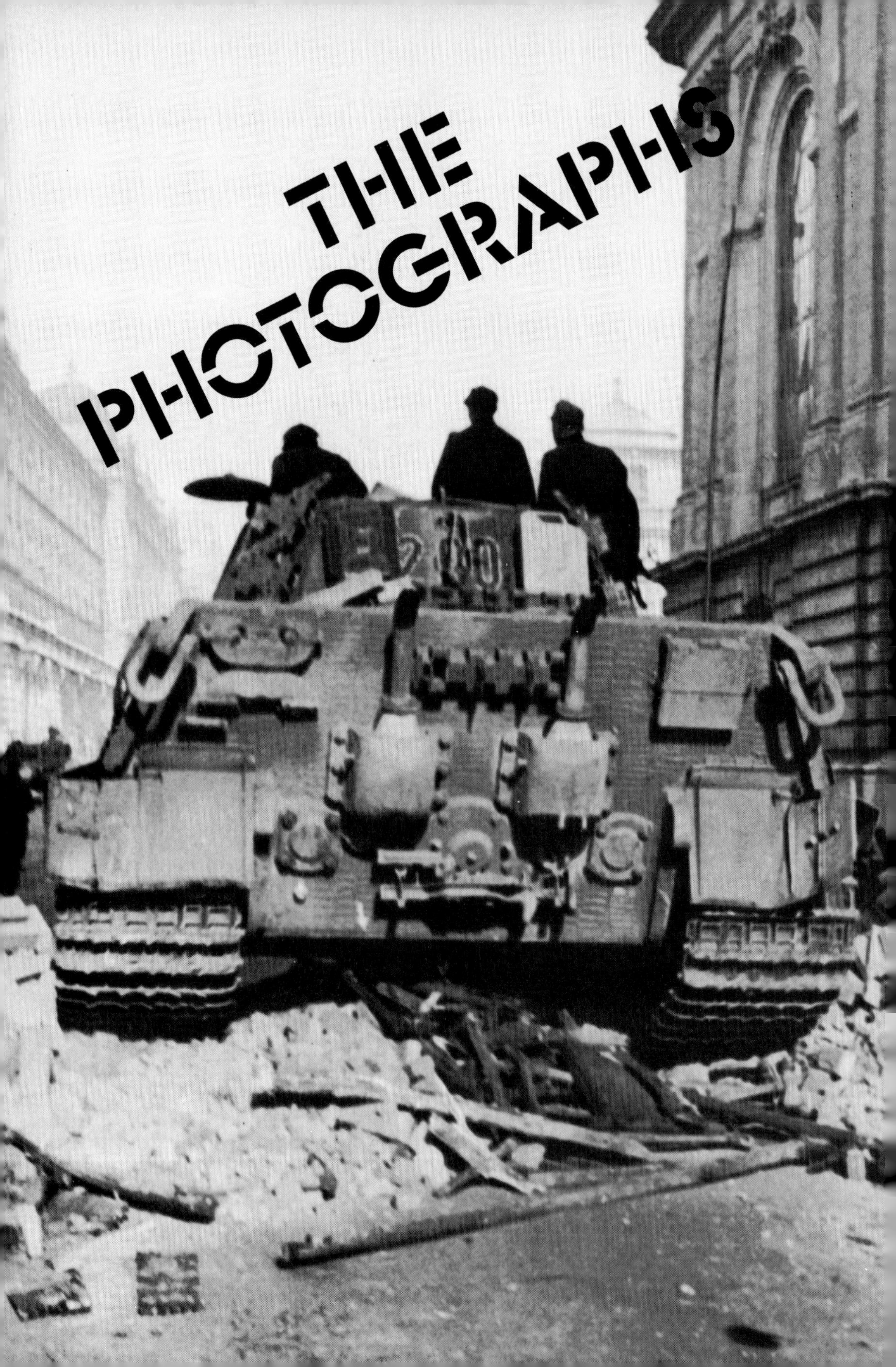

Left A Tiger II demolishes a barricade in Budapest, spring 1945 (680/8282a/32a).

Although several of the photographs on the ensuing few pages are thought to have been taken during the battle of Kursk, there is no guarantee that this is so. They do, however, show representative vehicles in similar terrain and at approximately the right time. **Above** Wehrmacht Panzer-Grenadiers in an SdKfz 251 follow tanks into battle through the long grass (323/2746/23a).

Below Sturmgeschütz IIIF of an unidentified Army unit (83/3361/13a).

Background photograph, insets above and below Replenishing the ammunition and topping up the fuel tanks of a Tiger I during a pause in the fighting (22/2948/37, 36 and 27).

Opposite page and above Pause for a drink of water for the crew of a Tiger I (22/2949/6,3 and 4).

Right and top of page 20 Two views of a 10th Panzer Division SdKfz 250 which must actually have been taken in 1941 or early 1942 as this formation was destroyed in Tunisia and never reformed. Nevertheless, two good pictures of this useful little vehicle (78/3059/18 and 19).

Above A PzKpfw V Panther Ausf D with early style cupola and an interesting camouflage scheme of dark green or red-brown over its basic dark yellow finish (705/264/1).

Below and below left Maintenance being carried out on a Tiger I alongside a Russian hut (22/2948/5 and 8).

Background photograph Panzer-Grenadiers in SdKfz 250 and 251 half-tracks supported by StuG IIIs move up during the battle of Kursk (243/2261/33).

Inset Army officers confer with Generaloberst Model within the safety of a trench (687/140/11).

Opposite page and above Externally, the PzKpfw V Ausf A differed principally from the earlier Ausf D in its revised cupola, while the Ausf G saw the replacement of the driver's visor by a periscope. The two vehicles left and above are Ausf As and Gs, those above left are Ds (88/3746a/27, 280/1096/15 and 12).

Right StuG III in a rather crude criss-cross camouflage scheme (22/2944/2).

Above PzKpfw IIFs seen from the turret hatch of another vehicle (78/3076/22a).
Below and below right PzKpfw IIIMs in the summer of 1943 showing an unusual camouflage scheme. Note that the foreground vehicle below right lacks spaced armour on its mantlet (219/595/23 and 19).

Above Even though it resembles the SS 'Totenkopf' Division's 'Kursk' marking, the three-barred device on this PzKpfw IVG is more likely to be that of some so-far unidentified unit although the date is right—summer 1943 (219/561a/15).

Above StuG IIIF descends a slope, accompanied by cavalry (78/3086/16).

Below Luftwaffe personnel with an SdKfz 251 and PzKpfw IIF. The NCO in the centre is an Oberfeldwebel (323/2746/11).

Above Routine work on a Tiger I. Note battered state of the mudguards! (22/2935/10a).

Below and over page Camouflaging Tiger Is against aerial observation on the edge of a wood. Despite their size, these vehicles could be made to 'disappear' in a very short space of time (22/2936/16, 17a and 21).

Above left Removing the turret of a Tiger by means of a Fries portable 33,000 lb gantry crane (278/875/30a).

Above right Working on the engine of one of the preceding Tigers (22/2936/27).

Below Working on a Tiger turret at a field workshop in a wood (695/405/36a).

Left An engine change under similar circumstances for a PzKpfw VG. The lifting vehicle is an SdKfz 9/2 half-track (280/1096/34).

Above Gunlayer and commander inside what I believe is a Tiger (709/321/18).

Below Can any reader positively identify this tank's interior? To me, it looks like a KV-I (82/3302/15a).

Above View from the turret of a PzKpfw IV (281/1104/29).
Below PzKpfw IVGs fording a stream (87/3680/8).

Above The crew of a StuG III with their best friend (88/3744a/18).
Below 5 cm Pak 38 on tow behind a light half-track (280/1058/12).

03

Inset left Early production PzKpfw IIIL mounting the new turret without side vision ports, but lacking spaced armour and retaining the lower hull escape hatches (78/3075/4).

Background photograph Later-production PzKpfw IIIL without escape hatches and with spaced armour. Note aerial recognition flag on background vehicle and logs laid across a muddy stretch of ground to facilitate movement (78/3076/10a).

Inset right Infantry follow behind a StuG III (78/3083/39).

Above PzKpfw IIIJ in the autumn of 1943 (323/2743/24).
Below PzKpfw III of the 16th Panzer-Grenadier Division, parent formation of the later 16th Panzer Division. The division's 'three-legged swastika' Trinacria can just be discerned on the rear plate (78/3070/21).

Above A well-camouflaged PzKpfw III, possibly of the 'Grossdeutschland' Division, shows its paces before a group of officers (230/686/17).

Below PzKpfw IVGs ford a shallow stream (87/3680/9).

Left StuG III commanders Fritz Auling and Herbert Schramm pose for the camera with their newly awarded Knight's Crosses (86/3574/5).

Below Refuelling a StuG III. I have been unable to discover the identity of the badge on the left of the hull rear (87/3671a/14).

Right StuG IIIs ford a stream. Unusually, the commander of the foreground vehicle is wearing a steel helmet, complete with camouflage cover (78/3086/17).

Below right PzKpfw IV on a dusty Russian road (87/3653/4).

Above Knocked-out Soviet T-34/76D which would make a good diorama subject, perhaps? (682/26/18).
Below Panzerjäger 38(t) Marder IIIs armed with the Russian 7·62 cm Pak 36(r) gun (22/2944/23).

Above Loading ammunition aboard a StuG IIIG (277/833/5a).
Below PzKpfw IIIMs in the midday sun (281/1104/27).

Opposite page and right StuG IIIBs with short-barrelled 7·5 cm StuK 37 L/24 guns (78/3064/3, 6 and 7).

Below PzKpfw IIIJ in south Russia (87/3654/8a).

Left Late-production Tiger I in whitewash camouflage despite the apparent thaw (701/364/36).

Below Another late Tiger; the badge on the turret side is, unfortunately, impossible to make out (278/885/24a).

Right A mounted despatch rider brings a message to the commander of a Nashorn (278/861/20).

Below right An armoured train, including the upper half of a PzKpfw 38(t) in its armament (700/254/4).

OVERLEAF

Background photograph Rare picture indeed of a staff car bearing an AOK pennant and the Crimea award shield, alongside a very dusty Tiger I, an early version with simple vision slits in the cupola and a pistol port on the left-hand turret side. Feiffel air cleaners are also fitted (705/262/11).

Inset PzKpfw VA, also in the Crimea (88/3746a/30).

WH-1405592

A 02

Above left Wehrmacht wargamers! Planning an operation with the help of a terrain model divided into 100-metre grid squares (83/3373/4).

Below Captured Russian T-34/76E (differing from the 76D shown on page 42 in having a commander's cupola) in service with the 'Grossdeutschland' Division (711/427/18).

Above right Grenadiers and a PzKpfw VA in the smoke of a burning village (695/408/29).

Right The crew of a PzKpfw IVG or H and their unsuspecting lunch! (87/3675a/29).

Background photograph SdKfz 251/16 mittlerer Flammpanzerwagen Ausf D in action (281/1110/2).

Inset above MG 34 position alongside a knocked-out T-34 which has been turned into a bunker (83/3380/16a).

Inset right German gunners with a Russian 76·2 mm Model 1941/SiS 3 field gun. This was a hybrid weapon of which few were produced, mounting a Model 1939 barrel with modified recoil mechanism and the addition of a muzzle brake on a 57 mm anti-tank gun chassis. In German hands these weapons were designated 7·62 cm FK 288/1(r) (687/134/6a).

Above A late production Tiger with an SdKfz 7 mounting quad 20 mm anti-aircraft guns. The 'camouflaged' material draped over the latter's bonnet is definitely non-issue! (90/3947/12).

Below StuG IIIF in the autumn of 1943 (83/3359/21).

Above A Nashorn bearing what appears to be a coat of arms on its mudguard, possibly a regimental or city crest (240/2145/11).

Below I would welcome identification of this vehicle from any reader; it does not appear to feature in any of my own reference books (81/3285/31).

Above Infantry in reversible winter clothing shelter beside a burned-out T-34/76E (277/839/13a).
Below A column of StuG IIIs in the bleak winter landscape (278/888/4).

Above PzKpfw IVG or possibly an Ausf H with the old type of idler (711/413/19).
Below PzKpfw IVH with Tigers in the background (227/843/6).

Above German paratrooper in fur-lined smock 'shoots up' a BT-7; the smile on his face and the fact that the smoke is coming from a canister reveal this to be a pure propaganda picture (555/903/32).
Below Stug IIIG with badly weathered whitewash camouflage (277/837/18).

Above Repairs to a Marder III. Note the 'kill' markings on the superstructure (241/2167/4).

Below A PzKpfw IVH moves past a group of infantry whose helmets, interestingly, have not been whitewashed (277/843/8).

Left Despite the snow, these two infantrymen wear their reversible clothing to display the splinter camouflage. The man in front carries an RPzB 43, the gas mask being for protection from the rocket's exhaust (279/942/24).

Below A Nashorn in convoy with wheeled and semi-tracked trucks (279/950/16).

Right Oberleutnant Dr Wilhelm Knouth, a Tiger company commander, with Knight's Cross. Note the throat microphone (278/873/25).

Below right A snow-covered T-34/76E moves past a PzKpfw IV whose front has been liberally covered with spare track links for added protection (277/836/12).

This page and above right Three good views of a Marder III crewed by Fallschirmjäger personnel. Its faded whitewash camouflage has been 'repainted' with liberal handfuls of mud! (560/1113/11, 32 and 8).

Below right PzKpfw IVH with zimmerit finish (277/843/30).

Left BMW motor cycle combination with warmly clad driver and passenger, and a crudely whitewashed Tiger in the background (279/946/20).

Below A pair of Hummels standing apparently abandoned in the snow (278/898/3).

Right Timbers creak as a Tiger crosses a wooden bridge (279/904/31).

Below right Good close-up of a Bergepanzer III, a turretless PzKpfw III used as a recovery and engineers' vehicle (278/883/33a).

Above Unusual picture of a 19·4 cm Kanone 485(f) GPF, a French heavy self-propelled gun impressed into German service on the Eastern Front (700/297/10a).

Below PzKpfw IVH of an unidentified unit. The badge on turret side and mudguard appears to consist of a black shield with a red(?), downward-pointing, barred arrow, although it is unclear even under a magnifying glass (701/356/28).

Above Grenadiers hitch a lift on a PzKpfw IV (89/3779/32a).

Below Roadside halt for a column of PzKpfw IVHs, while horse-drawn transport trundles in the opposite direction (90/3911/15).

Left A wounded Luftwaffe Oberleutnant anxiously scans the skies from his SdKfz 251 radio vehicle. In the background is a troop of PzKpfw IVGs (88/3710/15a).

Below left PzKpfw IVH and supporting infantry (700/272/17).

Right Wehrmacht Oberleutnant with Knight's Cross and four individual tank kill badges on his arm (85/3466/34).

Below A column of half-tracks with armoured bonnets and cabs move up past a PzKpfw VA; the foreground vehicle mounts a 20 mm anti-aircraft gun (90/3912/28a).

Background photograph Military signposts at a road junction in Kharkov (326/2869/29).

Inset Heavy armoured railway coach; several such would normally be coupled to make up a train (690/201/16).

Above PzKpfw IIIs loaded on to flatbed railway wagons at Orel station. This picture was probably taken much earlier in the campaign (327/2837/25).

Below PzKpfw IVH with extra track links liberally festooned around its front (690/201/30).

Above SdKfz 4/1 Maultier with ten 15 cm Nebelwerfer tubes (689/190/30).

Below Loading the Nebelwerfer tubes on the same vehicle (689/190/27).

Above Panther with dense 'camofoliage' (281/1104/32).

Below PzKpfw IIIJ fitted with spaced frontal armour and turret and hull schürzen, accompanied by PzKpfw IVHs (689/195/3).

Above PzKpfw IIIL in overall yellow finish plus a light dusting of snow (326/2864/18).

Below PzKpfw IVs move past infantry in foxholes, while a building burns in the background (690/201/34).

Above A captured Soviet SU-85 preceded by a StuG IV (703/472/20). **Below** A troop of Panthers on the march (696/432/2). **Above right** Good close-up of the zimmerit finish on a PzKpfw IVH (689/195/9). **Right** Knocked-out KV-85 heavy tank in the spring of 1944 (687/139/21a).

Above PzKpfw IVH at speed (281/1104/9).
Below A wounded tank crewman being eased on to a stretcher with the willing assistance of accompanying infantry (87/3667a/10a).

Above The hinged doors in the turret schürzen are open on this PzKpfw IV, something not often seen in photographs, but of more interest is the unusual camouflage scheme (711/421/5a).
Below Steyr RSO fully tracked truck towing a 5 cm Pak 38 (240/2130/5).

These pages and over page The Jagdpanther is often hailed as the best tank destroyer of the war, and its clean lines are well displayed in this sequence of photographs. The interior shot shows how comparatively spacious this vehicle was (717/17/12, 15, 17, 20, 22 and 721/396/13).

Fernhörer

Above Crews parade in front of an StuG IIIG whose individual number, 251, is repeated on the commander's cupola (239/2100/1).

Below StuG IIIF (81/3268/25a).

Left SdKfz 251 Ausf Ds. The badge on their rears resembles that of 20th Panzer Division, but with a downward sloping instead of an upright vertical arrow (696/438/9a).

Below left Panther's eye view. These both appear to be Ausf Gs (694/303/20).

Right StuG IIIF in wavy pattern camouflage (78/3083/36a).

Below A captured Soviet T-34/85-II followed by a Tiger whose number, 001, is painted on the gun barrel (694/303a/23a).

Above Loading wounded into an SdKfz 251/8 Ausf D which has a very unusual finish: zimmerit? In the background is a PzKpfw VA or G (240/2145/17a).

Below PzKpfw IIL (Luchs) in the autumn of 1944 (90/3931/19).

Above Half a dozen PzKpfw IVHs, all with zimmerit finish, the foreground vehicle bearing the personal name 'Hildegard' (689/195/33).

Below StuG IIIG and crew (687/142/28).

This page and right Three rare pictures of PzKpfw IVs said to have been taken during the breakout from the Cherkassy pocket (578/1945/23, 689/195/12 and 708/298/21).

Below right A well-whitewashed PzKpfw VD with an SdKfz 252 in the background (90/3918/11).

Above, opposite page and page 92 One of the rare sequences of photographs from the Bundesarchiv illustrating the closing stages of the war, these pictures show PzKpfw VIBs in Budapest in 1945 (680/8282a/3a, 16a, 9a, 38a and 18a).

Below A well-wrapped soldier in greatcoat and fur cap gnaws on a piece of frozen bread alongside an SdKfz 252 ammunition carrier (84/3416/16).

Right Budapest, spring 1945, although what this Waffen-SS grenadier and Hungarian infantryman have got to smile about defeats the imagination. Behind them is a Tiger II (PzKpfw VIB) with Henschel turret (680/8282a/17a).

APPENDIX

German tanks introduced into service 1943–45

PzKpfw II Ausf L Luchs The final development of the PzKpfw II series, the Luchs (Lynx) was produced between September 1943 and January 1944. It carried a crew of four, weighed 13 tons and was armed with a 20 mm KwK 38. Top speed was 60 km/h and endurance 290 km. Designed as a light reconnaissance tank, it had armour plate ranging from 10 to 30 mm in thickness.

PzKpfw III Ausf M Virtually identical with the Ausf L apart from repositioned smoke dischargers, fording equipment and, in some cases, wider tracks, the PzKpfw IIIM had a crew of five, weighed 22·7 tons and was armed with the 5 cm L/60 KwK 39. It had a speed and range of 40 km/h and 155 km respectively. Armour plate varied between 10 and 57 mm, most vehicles also being equipped with turret and side Schürzen.

PzKpfw III Ausf N Adapted from PzKpfw III J, L and M variants, the Ausf N differed significantly only in its armament, the short-barrelled 7·5 cm KwK L/24, which raised its weight to 23 tons. 700 were produced between June 1942 and August 1943.

PzKpfw IV Ausf H Manufactured between April 1943 and July 1944, this was essentially an up-armoured Ausf G with different suspension. It was crewed by five men, weighed 25 tons and was armed with the 7·5 cm KwK 40. Top speed was 38 km/h, ensurance 210 km, and armour plate between 10 and 80 mm thick.

PzKpfw IV Ausf J The last production version of the PzKpfw IV, of which 1,758 were manufactured between June 1944 and March 1945. Outwardly similar to the Ausf H, it featured slightly increased roof armour but the main difference was internal. The power traverse unit was replaced by hand-operated gear to save space for extra fuel, increasing its range to 320 km.

PzKpfw V Ausf D As stated in the introduction, this first Panther variant proved something of a disappointment when it was introduced to battle at Kursk. Based on lessons learned from study of the T–34, it featured exceptionally well-sloped armour plate in direct contrast with the almost vertical, 'boxy' shape of other German tanks. Weighing 43 tons, it was crewed by five men and mounted the long-barrelled 7·5 cm L/70 KwK 42 gun. Top speed was 46 km/h and endurance 200 km. Armour plate ranged from 16 to 100 mm in thickness, the 55 degree slope of the front plates adding to its protective value.

PzKpfw V Ausf A Produced from August 1943 to May 1944, during which time 2,000 vehicles were built, the Ausf A contained many modifications incorporated as a result of experience with the Ausf D. Pistol ports were eliminated, a much-improved commander's cupola and ball-mounted bow machine-gun installed, and modifications made to the wheels and engine cooling system to improve reliability. Mantlet armour was increased to 110 mm and the weight rose to 44·8 tons.

PzKpfw V Ausf G The final production version of the Panther, of which 3,126 were produced from March 1944 to April 1945, the Ausf G had a redesigned hull with increased armour protection. The driver's visor was replaced by a periscope and many minor mechanical changes incorporated to improve reliability. Weight rose to 45.5 tons.

PzKpfw VI Ausf B The Tiger II, or Königstiger (King Tiger), was the last German tank design to enter production. It evolved through a desire to have a heavy tank capable of carrying the long-barrelled 8·8 cm L/71 KwK 43, and both Henschel and Porsche submitted prototypes. The Henschel design won although the Porsche turret was installed on the first 50 Tiger IIs. This heavy tank weighed 68 tons and had a crew of five but was grossly underpowered, being fitted with the same engine as in the much lighter Panther. This still produced a surprising top speed of 35 km/h and a range of 170 km. The most striking feature of the tank was its well-sloped and immensely strong armour plate, from 40 to 180 mm in thickness, which rendered it all but impervious to any anti-tank gun in existence, certainly from the front. 489 were produced from January 1944 to March 1945.

Other titles in the same series

No 1 Panzers in the desert
by Bruce Quarrie

No 2 German bombers over England
by Bryan Philpott

No 3 Waffen-SS in Russia
by Bruce Quarrie

No 4 Fighters defending the Reich
by Bryan Philpott

No 5 Panzers in North-West Europe
By Bruce Quarrie

No 6 German fighters over the Med
by Bryan Philpott

No 7 German paratroops in the Med
by Bruce Quarrie

No 8 German bombers over Russia
by Bryan Philpott

No 9 Panzers in Russia 1941–43
by Bruce Quarrie

No 10 German fighters over England
by Bryan Philpott

No 11 U-boats in the Atlantic
by Paul Beaver

In preparation

No 13 German bombers over the Med
by Bryan Philpott

No 14 German capital ships
by Paul Beaver

No 15 German mountain troops
by Bruce Quarrie

No 16 German fighters over Russia
by Bryan Philpott

No 17 E-boats and coastal craft
by Paul Beaver

No 18 German maritime aircraft
by Bryan Philpott

No 19 Panzers in the Balkans and Italy
by Bruce Quarrie

No 20 German destroyers and escorts
by Paul Beaver